Entrepreneur's Personal Branding Handbook

The Top 10 Personal Branding Tools & Resources For
Entrepreneurs To Build Their Influence & Dominate Their
Market In Rapid Time & Without Spending A Fortune.

Richard Janes

The Big Idea
Behind This Little Book.

Entrepreneurs (i.e. you) are busy people - crazy busy people. You're already working long hours, and while you know that building your brand recognition will lead to greater opportunities and more interesting projects in your chosen market, the idea of sitting down and trying to form a plan all on your own seems like a massive time suck. You need a quick solution.

This book is that solution. It can give you, the entrepreneur, a set of tools to quickly brand yourself and start seeing results. It provides a set of tools that will help you on your journey to becoming one of the go-to thought leaders/experts in your niche.

Just think of what you could achieve with a better known voice and an increase in demand for your expertise - that's what we are talking about when we dive into personal brand building.

But before we dive into the book, it's important that you and I get on the same page about what personal branding is and why it's so important.

A brand, whether corporate or personal, is the sum of everything that the brand does/is involved with. Disney's brand is just as much about the iconic three circles that children all over the world point to and shout 'Mickey Mouse,' as it is about the feeling of dread that's evoked when you think about spending two hours in line at one of their theme parks.

Branding isn't just about logos, colors, business cards, and letter heads, it's about the feeling that the brand gives people. What comes to your mind when you think about Barack Obama, Richard Branson, Oprah Winfrey, Sheryl Sandberg, the headmaster of your middle school, your first boss, your first lover?

Everything that comes to mind is a part of their brand. It's a set of distinguishing elements, experiences, and visual cues that are able to be remembered by others, and it impacts whether they draw someone in or push them away.

Given this definition, we all have a brand whether we like it or not. We all have a set of distinguishing elements, experiences and visual cues that are able to be remembered by others, and yet so few of us take the time to think about the impression we are making. So few of us put the effort into planning how we communicate with the world, on both a conscious and subconscious level, so as to leave impressions that will open up more opportunities for us to shine doing what we do best. So many of us don't proactively build our personal brand. But if your brand is getting defined whether you like it or not, doesn't it make more sense to proactively influence the process?

I used to think personal brands were just for celebrities. In fact, I built my career around it after becoming Hollywood's go-to personal brand builder in 2010. Very quickly my client list swelled to include names ranging from talk show host Larry King and America's Toughest Trainer Jillian Michaels through, to Olympic Athletes and basketball players with the LA Lakers.

I've provided brand building strategies for heads of state, globally known recording artists, and New York Times best-selling authors. Over the last nine years, my team and I have helped to grow over 100,000,000 fans across social media - fans that have helped positively position my clients so they could further their career and provide true value to their partners.

Then, in 2016, things took a turn for the worse, and it had me reassess the idea that real personal brand building wasn't just for those that wanted to be celebrities.

The agency I had developed to service all these celebrities was growing at an unprecedented pace, and I found that I'd been sucked into the role of company executive. I was stuck in finance meetings, contract negotiations, dealing with HR issues, and the world of venture capital.

We'd split the agency in two so that we could spin out a technology company that was already powering 90% of the live television chats that TV actors were having with audiences on Facebook and Twitter, and we were trending globally most weeks - if you've ever seen a celebrity live chatting on social media around a TV broadcast, be that George Lopez or Tim Tebow with the Superbowl, or the cast of Glee, Pretty Little Liars, Scandal, True Detective, The Walking Dead, (insert your favorite TV show here) that was most likely my company making that happen.

As the organization grew, I found that more and more of my time was spent away from my own zone of genius. I found myself spending hours and hours dealing with computer programmers who were based in time zones all over the world who were missing their deadlines by weeks, then months, and ultimately an entire year! This 'top' tech team was introduced to me by our lead venture investor who kept assuring us that everything would be alright - that these guys were the best - even though each delivery had so many bugs and errors that it rendered the build useless. The delays were causing us a MASSIVE cashflow strain as we burnt through our entire runway.

Looking up one day, I realized that I had traveled so far away from my origin - an origin of one-to-one contact with artists where we sought to build their brand by getting to the crux of the unique value they offer the world. An origin of helping people take giant leaps towards their big audacious hairy goals. An origin where I got up in the morning and actually looked forward to what I would be doing.

Have you ever had a moment where you looked up and asked yourself "how on earth did I get 'here' when I was aiming for over 'there!?!'" In some cases, it's not that where you are is necessarily a bad thing, but it's not where you thought you would be, where perhaps you could really shine and make an impact on the world.

It all came to a head when, on a blazing hot Los Angeles summer afternoon, I suddenly fell ill and found myself being raced along Hollywood Boulevard to the emergency room.

Ninety minutes later, having been stabilized, I was in a hospital gown sitting in a sterile examination room waiting for the doctor with nothing but the echoing sound of the wall clock ticking to stretch out of the wait.

What proceeded was a series of events that had me sit up and realize that the root of my problem was misalignment. I was stuck wearing a hat that I had no business wearing. I had lost myself following the path of 'bigger is better' and 'more money means more success,' and I had become reactive to opportunities vs proactive. The opportunities were huge, there is no doubt, but just because an opportunity is huge doesn't mean that I'm the right person to take it.

I go into the whole story behind this major life changing moment in the first episode of my podcast series, 'Finding Passion & Purpose' which you can check out on Apple Podcasts, but the outcome of this chapter in my life was the realization that I had to get back to my zone of genius. That I had to be PROACTIVE with my life, and start putting myself out there in a way that would attract not just any opportunities, but the right opportunities. Opportunities where I could really shine and build the career and life that served me, my family, the community around me, and the world at large, at my very best. As I had this realization, it dawned on me that this was exactly the same starting point that I took my celebrity clients to when we sat down to discuss building their brands: 'How do I start proactively communicating with the world to open up more suitable opportunities to do what I do best.'

I took a deep breath and wondered if all the behind the scenes tools and resources I had employed to help build my celebrity clients careers could actually be applied to my own. The goal wasn't celebrity status, but rather to return me to what I do best and to make a big enough mark on the world so that if there was anyone out their contemplating building their personal brand I would be top of their list to reach out to. The goal was niche domination.

Within a month of deploying the tools and resources that I am about to share with you now, my career had taken a massive leap forward. I had to take the heart breaking step to close the technology company I'd been working so hard to build (still with the developers unable to deliver a final product), I'd managed to take a back seat at the agency, leaving it to be run by a team that loved the executive work that was required of them, and I had replaced my agency income with a hand full of non-celebrity clients that included a lawyer, a screenwriter, a yoga instructor, a therapist, a realtor, and the CEO of a publicly traded company. All these non-celebrity clients, just like myself, started to see big leaps forward in brand awareness around their zone of genius, and with this increased level of brand awareness, came incoming calls, more refined opportunities, and riches that could only be gained by getting laser focused on their niches.

Since that time, my career has continued to grow stronger and stronger; all as a result of doubling down on my personal brand.

Now it's time for you to do the same.

So here we go...

The ten tools and resources I am about to introduce you to are used each week by my team and I, together with the thousands of entrepreneurs, just like you, who stepped up to the plate and enrolled in my personal brand challenges built to unlock the true power of you personal brand.

These tools and resources work across every industry and cater to any personal brand goals that you might be working towards. If you have any doubt that this will work for you just go to my Facebook page, post a comment telling me what you do for a living/want to be doing, and someone from my team (or I) will jump in and tell you how building your brand will provide you with massive benefits!

The ten tools that we are going to be looking at in this book are not the exhaustive list that I make available through my personal brand challenges, nor do they help you develop a firm foundation from which to grow your brand - both of these would need much more time than we have available in this handbook.

What these tools represent are my go-to, get-out-the-gate-fast methods that can help you to start hitting a good string of singles that can help you win at the game of personal brand building, and they break down into the following areas:

1. Outsourcing Your Brand Building
2. Content Creation & Inspiration
3. Reaching Your Audience

Now there are two main objections people make to getting started with brand building. The first is time, and the second is money.

As far as time, the tools I am about to walk you through are intended to be embraced quickly and experimented with on a trial and error basis. In my experience this is the best way to approach anything. Jump in, get it wrong, learn how to use the tools in a way that suits you best, and reap the benefits while your competition is still umming and ahhhing about the 'best' way to move forward. These tools will speed up the path to achieving your goals if you just get out of your own way and use them!

As far as money is concerned, for most of us in the west, money is a priority not a resource, and with today's global economy, you don't have to invest a small fortune to build your brand. I've purposefully built this resource list in such a way that many brand building tasks can be outsourced for the price of a cup of coffee or a meal out at a restaurant. Remember, money is a priority not a resource.

Now there's a ton more you can do above and beyond utilizing these ten tools and resources, but start with these, and you'll be well on your way. If you want to go deeper, I'd welcome you to join one of my personal brand challenges, and I'll let you in on how you can do that once we get to the tenth and final resource.

Regardless of us working more closely together, these tools will make a difference in your life IF you take the proactive step to start using them. What's the famous quote from Zig Ziglar? "When we change the input in our minds, we change the output in our lives." I like this a lot but I think there's a little something missing. I believe it should be "When we change the input - and take proactive action around it - we change the output in our lives."

Get ready to take some proactive action.

Outsourcing Your Brand Building

One of the things I struggled with as I built my agency was managing my staff. I'm a useless manager. I hate keeping tabs on people and the constant circling back to see where they are with a project, and if they are hitting any roadblocks.

Additionally, as a start up, you're often in a position where each employee has a long list of tasks they're responsible for. I would find that some of my staff were really good in a few areas and then the rest of the tasks would be glossed over quickly, or worse, not tended to at all. As these staff members were performing parts of their jobs well, I wasn't going to replace them and, as I've already established, I wasn't good at managing them to round out their results.

I think this can also be applied to ourselves.

Each of us as entrepreneurs have a long list of tasks that we are responsible for. There are some tasks that we do really well and a ton we don't give the proper attention to. They always end up at the bottom of the list even if we know they have the ability to make a material difference. Some of us try to farm these tasks on to the people around us who are equally unsuited to the job. Some of us never address these short comings and wonder why our career is stalling, or why we are not living up to our true potential.

All this changed for me with outsourcing.

Before you close off and say "outsourcing won't work for me", or "I can't afford to hire anyone", which is the response of 60% of my private clients, let me categorically and unequivocally tell you that this can work for you. The results and opportunity cost for doing so, even if you already have a team for other areas of your business, are incredible - and it doesn't have to cost an arm and a leg!

The two platforms I use the most for outsourcing are Fiverr and Upwork. We'll dive into each platform and how I use them in just a moment, but the common link between the two are that they both allow me to source extremely skilled niche service providers for a very low cost. The end result is that I have anywhere from 10-20 people working for me at any one time for less than a full time member of staff. Additionally, as each person only has one or two things to do, it's very easy for me to hold them accountable for their results. If someone is under performing, I can change them up really quickly without an impact on my main business, as I have built in redundancies.

Before we dive into how I use these platforms, let's breakdown how each platform works and what makes them different from the others.

Upwork

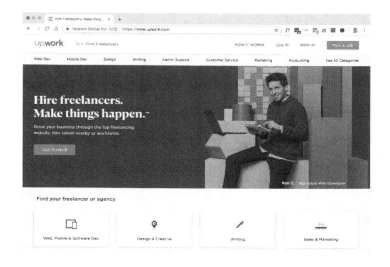

Upwork is my go-to platform for outsourcing work. What I love about this platform is that global freelancers 'apply' to be awarded your job. All you do is fill in a brief job description of what you need to have done, give a budget (either a flat rate or a maximum hourly rate), and wait for the applications to flow in. The more precise you can be the better but don't worry about getting it perfect, as that will slow you down. If you have something that needs doing it should take you no more than 5 minutes to get the job listed and for applications to start flooding in.

You'll find all sorts of talent at Upwork. In the last 3 months I have contracted Upwork freelancers to do the following tasks and paid the following amounts:

- Creating animated gifs for social media. ($5-10 each)
- Copywriting checks on Facebook Ads ($15 per hour)
- Entering 1,000 coupon codes into a spreadsheet for printing ($3.25 per hour)
- Proofreading a 1,500 word article within the next 2 hours ($25 per hour - paid $12.50)
- A scheduling assistant to help manage my crazy schedule ($25 per hour)
- Photo retouching artist ($3 per hour)
- Ebook cover mockup ($5 each)
- Creating a custom font from my handwriting ($25 flat rate)
- Programming my new website ($25 per hour)

- Graphic designer for social media posts ($10 per hour)
- Online course research ($4 per hour)
- Transcribing my podcasts ($5 per hour)
- Logo design ($20 each)
- Illustrations for a book ($12.50 per hour)
- Editing my podcast ($25 per hour)

Now as with any outsourcing, the quality of applicants varies greatly, and while some provide links to amazing portfolios, you can never fully guarantee that they actually did the work. The best way to filter Upwork freelancers is by looking at their reviews. Even then, you can end up with a dud.

How I work around this is to hire 2-3 freelancers to do each job, giving them one hour to prove themselves. After that hour, I then review their work and select the freelancer I wish to move forward with.

Once I've found a reliable freelancer who produces great work they become my go-to for that very specific task. Sometimes I can use them once a week, and sometimes it can go six months before I have a new task for them.

Upwork has a fantastic system for monitoring freelancers who are billing per hour. For freelancers to get paid they have to log the time that they start the work and log out when they complete the work (or whenever they take breaks). The Upwork desktop app then takes a series of six snapshots of their screen per hour to prove that they are actually working and not just watching Netflix or surfing social media to run up your hours. It also records the total number of mouse clicks, scroll actions, and keystrokes per segment. With this fantastic piece of technology, there is no need for me to 'manage' the freelancer or worry about them inflating their hours. All I have to do is assess the end result. A results driven workforce? Sounds cool, huh?

Below you can see what the time log dashboard looks like from a hiring standpoint. This particular job is for the audio editing of my speakers reel, and Alex (whom I engage with to edit and mix all my podcasts) is a digital nomad from Argentina. He just travels the world picking up jobs on Upwork, and he is fantastic. I think he edited this audio from a beach in Bali.

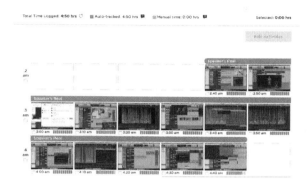

Upwork's use of the time log monitoring software, combined with the fact that I can pay for Upwork jobs with my American Express Card (earning those lovely points) means that the process is simple - Upwork also takes care of all the taxes and paperwork. I've even found local freelancers who have come and worked alongside me at one of my offices in Los Angeles, Dallas, or Oklahoma City for a few days - and rather than getting them to sign paperwork and pay them directly, I set them up through Upwork with a simple click of a button.

What type of freelancers can I not find on Upwork?

While you can search for freelancers who live near you, Upwork wouldn't be my go-to for anything that requires someone to actually be in the office with me or for photographers, videographers, or voice over artists. When I say 'be in the office with me,' I'm talking about tasks such as sticking printed codes on brochures for an event or welcoming guests for my podcast recording sessions. Things where there is a real physical reason that the task can't be done remotely, not just because I prefer to have someone close.

The two platforms I use for these sorts of projects are Fiverr and Craigslist.

Fiverr

Fiverr was founded in 2010 with an extremely simple concept: freelancers can offer a service, or as they call it, a "gig", and charge someone $5. Given the restriction to $5, the freelancers that initially signed up to the service offered very simple tasks, but don't let the idea of a 'simple' task fool you. Simple for an accomplished freelancer might be extremely difficult for you. Additionally, through purchasing power parity (a fancy way of saying it's cheaper to buy something in one place than it is in another) $5 to someone in India is the equivalent of paying between $16-$20 in the US.

Some of the top tasks sold on Fiverr include:

- Graphic designs (Logos, business cards, letterheads, flyers, infographics)
- Keyword research for search engine optimization (for your blog and website)
- Voice over artists (for podcasts or hold music on your conference line)
- Whiteboard animation videos & video logo reveals

Personally I use this platform mainly for voice over artists (because Upwork doesn't have voice talent), and occasionally very basic graphic design if I come across a designer where their work jumps out at me. For example, for my son's eighth birthday, my ten year old daughter paid $5 to a cartoonist on Fiverr to produce a graphic poster in the style of Pokemon with my son battling alongside Pikachu, and it blew him away!

The big difference between Fiverr and Upwork is that rather than have hundreds of freelancers bid on your project, with Fiverr you search through their freelancers and select someone to do the work you want. This puts the onus on you to find great talent, and it can take a while to find great ones. The platform has grown quite considerably since it's early beginnings and while the $5 per job can still be found, many freelancers now start at $25 and have a number of addons for additional extras.

If you are thinking that you would never need a voiceover artist as you don't have a podcast, then what about your office voicemail system or conference line? Personally, I hate it when people share the free conference call numbers, it just reeks of laziness to me. At the agency we use Turbo Bridge, which costs just $9.95 per month. We get a dedicated conference number, and I then get a Fiverr voice over artist to record our greeting and hold music where we can tell the conference call participants about how great we are and how they'd be mad not to work with us. We constantly get comments from prospective clients about how much they learned about our company as they waited for the call to start.

Last but not least, the final platform I use to assist me in finding team members that I can contract is Craigslist.

Craigslist

If you are reading this and are located anywhere but the US, it may not be Craigslist you use but a localized version thereof. Essentially, Craigslist is an online classifieds platform just like the back pages of a newspaper used to be years ago where people would list both services offered and services wanted together with various things they wanted to sell. In England, the biggest platform is Gumtree. In Germany it is probably a site called Quoka. Just type "online classifieds" and your country name into Google to find a platform for your area.

For the sake of this handbook we'll use Craigslist as my go-to platform.

On this site, I regularly post gigs for photographers and videographers to help me gather social media content or film courses, speeches, or follow me at events such as the time Success Magazine interviewed me for their online "Success Academy" down in Dallas.

Just as with Upwork, my approach to these hires is to engage people for a short 1-hour job, usually paying a low rate that presents little risk to me so that I can see how they perform. If I like their work, then I will add them to my list and call on them as needed.

Because I test everyone out before asking them to work for me, I'm not too worried about professional experience and rely more on their portfolio and attitude. This enables me to give up-and-coming photographers and videographers an opportunity. I tend to pay between $100-$200 for an afternoon's photoshoot and between $200-$400 for videographers, including gear.

The rule I make for all photographers and videographers is that the work they do for me is work for hire, (which means I own all the rights), and I get all the footage they shoot at the end of the session - often downloaded onto my hard drive that I can take home with me. Many photographers will not work like this as they want to retain ownership. That doesn't work for me at the level of service I need, as I don't want to have to pay over and over again for use in different mediums -so if someone doesn't agree to work for hire, it is a swift pass.

Outsourcing through these channels is how I engage 90% of the team I have around me. The remaining 10% come from professionals I have built up a relationship with for many years and I am happy to pay a premium for, or in a few very specific cases, contract not as a work-for-hire but with an intended use such as a book cover or front cover of a magazine, and we have a clearly defined contract in place BEFORE we work together.

With any classified services, I do recommend that as you meet these people for the first time, you meet them in a public place where you can get to know them first. Never meet them in their home (or yours) unless of course they have a bonafide business address such as a photography studio, and always tell someone where you are going and who you are meeting with - better yet, bring someone with you.

So those are my three go-to platforms for assembling a fantastic team who can help you realize your vision at a fraction of the cost of hiring people full-time, and it will be so much more productive than relying on people you know who you are asking favors from or asking to step outside their zone of genius.

As Steve Jobs once said "Great things in business are never done by one person. They're done by a team of people."

So, what I hope I have established here is that you don't need to spend a fortune to get a team around you, and that you can hire a large team of niche experts - only using them at the right moment vs employing a small number of generalists that can't fully get you what you need.

With each of these platforms, I've found two great ways to manage results that take a little bit of time on the front end but earn dividends down the line.

The first is checklists.

Checklists are a great way to help new contractors stay on task and avoid unwanted confusion. Almost every process can be reduced to a series of steps that will ensure task completion without constant supervision - think of them like a safety net. By producing checklists for your tasks it also means that it's a lot easier to change up team members and for them to produce consistent results.

The second thing I do an awful lot is record videos. I do this to explain what I want done and to deliver feedback. I find it so much quicker than typing something out, and the team member can constantly go back and check the task.

If you can turn a computer on you can record a video of your computer screen - it really is that simple and only requires a few steps.

Apple Mac using Quicktime (which comes with your computer):

Step 1: Launch QuickTime.

Step 2: Select File and choose New Screen Recording.

Step 3: Click the small, white down arrow next to the record button and make sure "Internal Microphone" is enabled.

Step 4: Click the red record button.

Step 5: Click anywhere on the screen to start recording.

PC using Powerpoint (which probably came with your computer):

Step 1: Launch Powerpoint.

Step 2: Go to the Insert tab and click Screen Recording.

Step 3: In the dock that appears, click Select Area or use the keyboard shortcut Windows key + Shift + A. Using the crosshairs tool that appears, click and drag to select the part of your screen you want to record.

By default, both the audio and mouse pointer are recorded with powerpoint.

I've found that recording videos makes things so much simpler, especially when using talented freelancers through Upwork where English might not be their first language.

Whether you decide to conduct your search locally or globally, you will likely receive multiple responses to your advertisement. Many of my clients are worried about using non-native speakers to take on projects, but my advice to them is not to worry unless it's for writing services. My go-to team are from all over the world, including the Philippines, Croatia, Pakistan, Brazil, Canada, and of course, the good old US of A.

As far as communication goes with all these talented people from across the globe, I have the Upwork mobile app on my phone. The app has a chat functionality, much like a text message, so I can go back and forth with my team as needed. My phone will ping me whenever they have questions, so it's amazingly simple and enables me to feel that progress is being made even when I am sitting at the lake reading a good book!

The last two points I will make on outsourcing through these platforms before we move on to Inspiration and content, is that a.) you should always try to factor in buffer room, and b.) always pay promptly.

With buffer room I will often say I need the project done in five days when I really need it done in seven. This way, if they are late, or if you have to edit or send the work back for revisions, you will still be able to complete the project on time. Sometimes it isn't possible to build in buffers. I've had many projects that I needed done within 60 minutes and I post this in a title: *Blog Proofread In The Next 60 Minutes.*

Lastly, if you want your workers to be reliable and produce quality work, you need to be reliable too. This holds true in terms of project communication, as well as prompt payment. I'm sure you don't like not getting paid on time and neither does your freelancer. If they have to wait a long time for payment, they will not be as willing to produce quality work for you - and on a platform such as Upwork where both the freelancer and you as an employer get rated, it can start to impact the quality of your applicants if you pay late. When you're reliable and pay on time, you make them happy, they will be more eager to work with you, and will be more likely to produce high-quality work. We all know this but sometimes we forget.

Content Creation & Inspiration

A rather splendid chap called Mark Twain, you may have heard of him, once said:

"Substantially, all ideas are second-hand, consciously and unconsciously drawn from a million outside sources, and daily use by the garnerer with a pride and satisfaction born of the superstition that he originated them; whereas there is not a rag of originality about them anywhere except the little discoloration they get from his mental and moral calibre and his temperament, and which is revealed in characteristics of phrasing."

I'm in 100% in agreement with this argument. Our output is very much defined by our input, both consciously and subconsciously. It is through this lens that I approach design and content creation.

Twenty years ago, when you set out to create your logos, business cards, letterheads etc., you'd have to contract with a local designer who would listen to what you were wanting and then sit down and come up with a few ideas to show you. If any of them resonated, the designer would then work on them some more until you were happy. Today, this can cost you thousands of dollars. I've been there and done that. Some designers delivered amazing work, some completely missed the mark.

If you know a great fancy designer, and have the money to pay them, then great - but even if you're in this situation, I strongly recommend that you refer to the following steps as it will help guide your designer and projects to much better results.

What I'm a big proponent of is design and content templates. Now this is where I often hear the argument that your brand assets (logo, etc.) should be unique to you and your brand. The argument goes that you can't achieve a unique identity by using templates and pre-made logos that you buy off a website, as other people will be using the same logo. People will say that if you are doing this 'properly' and presenting a 'professional' image, you need to have a designer do something custom for you.

To this, I point people towards Mark Twain's quote and then ask them to comment on a number of big brand logos.

Let's first take a   look at Gucci and Chanel. Both brands are in the luxury market, they primarily target women, and have remarkably similar logos.

Gucci and Chanel

Then there's PayPal and Pandora, who are clearly in completely different markets, and yet have ended up confusing a lot of their loyal customers through similar logo updates.

Adolfo
@adolfo_lujano

I have PayPal and Pandora next to eachother and they look the same so whenever I want to go on Pandora I always end up clicking PayPal

♡ 8   2:58 PM · Feb 25, 2017

The moral of the story here is that even if you spend tens of thousands of dollars on the most fancy design companies (as I am sure these brands did), there will probably be very similar logos to the one they come up with already out there being used somewhere in this big bad world - and if there isn't, there probably will be one soon.

Now that we agree that going with a designer isn't necessarily going to give you a one-of-a-kind unique graphic, I want to introduce you to two platforms that I use to speed up my design process and save me a ton of money. Once I've pulled back the curtain on design, I then want to pull back the curtain on blog templates, email newsletters and books - what, you mean I don't have to write all my content from scratch?!?!? You betcha!"

CreativeMarket.com

Creative Market is a somewhat addictive design hub with premade fonts, graphics, web design themes, powerpoint slides, stock photography - the list goes on, and on. They have over 3.4 million products listed for sale with most assets coming in between $5-$49.

I suggest that many of my clients grab a cup of tea and put thirty minutes aside to look through the site for inspiration whenever they need something designed.

Envato.com

The other online design hub I use with equal regularity is Envato. I tend to find that some of their designs can look a little more rudimentary so you have to dig a little deeper to find the gold. Additionally, Envato have video templates that you can use for showreels etc., and make your work look like it has been produced by a top Hollywood production house.

For anyone who is having to produce designed assets constantly, you can sign up to Envato Elements which costs just $16.50 and gives you unlimited downloads to over 1.3 million assets. Wowzers!

idplr.com

If you've never heard of PLR content then your mind is about to be blown! Just as the previously named sites enable you to pay a small price to gain access to graphic elements for the right to edit or modify, PLR covers written content.

If you've always thought about writing a book, a blog, or newsletter but could never find the time or struggled with the content, then this is for you. PLR stands for Private Label Rights and covers a whole industry of online markets where you can purchase pre-written content and put your name on it.

Need a series of blogs on healthy living, team building, dental care, relationships, yoga, or entrepreneurism (anything really), then conduct a quick search on any of the top PLR providers. While idplr.com is one of the leaders within the space, you can also search for quality PLR content through forums like the Warrior Forum's "Warrior Special Offer" section where customer reviews will tell you whether or not the PLR content for sale is good quality. Two things I would recommend against, is buying out-of-date PLR content, or the mega article packs where they give you 10,000 articles for next to nothing! Many of these crazy, low-priced deals with an exorbitant amount of deliverables are comprised of barely intelligible content that is just going to slow you down.

So, why bother with PLR?

Time!

Let's take blogging as an example, you have a 434% higher chance of being ranked highly on search engines if you feature a blog as part of your website. Most of us know that it makes a massive difference and yet we fail to produce a regular blog that's going to attract all that lovely traffic to us. I get it though, I was in this position too! One of the biggest time sucks is working out what you are going to blog about and how to structure it. With PLR content, everything is done for you.

So do you just buy a pack of 24 blog posts for $20 and set them to post one per month on your website??? I would suggest not. A viable alternative is to use one of the template services I talk about on the following pages.

Using Templates.

There are three ways to use these services, and depending on the importance of what you are working on, there is a method that will be best suited. The three ways are:

1. Downloading, making no changes, and using.
2. Downloading, making minor changes and using.
3. Downloading, using as an inspiration, and creating your own version.

Downloading, making no changes, and using.

It's very rare that you can use this method with graphics and design work, as you'll want to feature your brand in some form or change the text. In many cases the license for using the content requires you to make a small adjustment for it to be used anyway - this is not the case with PLR content. You could download an e-book complete with a title and designed front cover and offer it for sale on your website tomorrow.

You're even able to put your name on these works as the author. For full disclosure, that is not what I did with this ebook - I'm currently sitting by the pool in Los Angeles typing this out freestyle in one very long sitting! I'll then send the google doc over to one of my Upwork proofreaders to tidy up and expand on certain sections. There wasn't a book like this available anywhere, which is why I'm writing it now!

But I digress.

If you find an ebook that matches your own philosophy and speaks to your niche, then this can be a great way to create a free giveaway product in return for someone giving you their email address (just check on the licensing of the ebook that you can give it away for free, in most cases you can, but it is worth checking). If you are interested in building your email list and working out how you can build a sales funnel around the value you have to offer, I'll touch on that with the last resource.

One type of PLR content that I recommend you DO NOT just download and use, is blog content. Why? Google, that's why!

Google favors unique content, so if you are using a PLR blog post that is available all over the web, it won't do you any favors in search ranking - if it's not going to help you in search, then what should you do? We'll get to that in a moment.

Downloading, making minor changes and using.

This is really for the graphics, logos etc. that you buy from CreativeMarket and Envato. With these, you'll want to change your name, perhaps adjust some colors etc., to match your own brand palette or take out a few elements that don't work for you. To do this, simply purchase the template and then head on over to Upwork and ask designers to bid on the changes you need. With logos, this can be done for as little as $5. For a multi-page presentation where there is a lot of text to change up or images that need to be switched out you can expect to spend more.

For design work, this option tends to be my go-to approach to getting audience-ready content turned around within 24 hours.

Downloading, using as an inspiration, and creating your own version.

With designed assets, you can assemble a few different pieces thats you like, find a designer whose work you like on Upwork or Fiverr (or a great designer you know if you want to go down that route), and then show them the designs and give them direction based on what you would like the final product to be.

Traditionally, this will get you to an end result that you are happy with a lot faster than sending a designer off to do what they 'think' will work well for your goals. I also do this with photographers, where I keep a Pinterest board of images that I like so that I can ask them to capture photos in a similar style to the reference images. (You can check out my personal brand photograph inspiration boards on Pinterest, just search Richard Janes).

With PLR content, this approach is where you make something unique to you, inspired by the PLR article, so that the Google gods can smile upon your website and send you some lovely traffic.

In this scenario, once you've found some great PLR content, you should put it all in a file and then find a copywriter/ghostwriter that you like on Upwork (or you can do this yourself). Ask the freelancer to read the article and then write a new version which emulates the original content, but uses your words. The goal is to add your own voice to the article so that it sounds like it's from you (which a good ghost writer should be able to do after reading a short selection of your work). Just make sure that at a minimum 30-50% of the content has a materially different sentence and paragraph structure than the purchased article.

Typically, good PLR authors write content based around profitable niche keywords and information that people in that niche are actively seeking. Identify what those keywords are, make sure that they are still included in your version, and purchasing that PLR article/ebook/newsletter will have saved you a ton of time in searching for this information yourself. Essentially, you are using their insights and PLR content as research sources that you use as the framework your own writing.

For those of you who still feel a little funny about using PLR content and templates in any way, think back to any celebrity autobiography that you've read. Do you really think that they wrote that, or do you think they used a ghostwriter for at least some of it? And don't be fooled into thinking you don't see design templates used widely across magazines, newspapers and billboards all over the world, too - they're everywhere!

Take 10 minutes now and type in "your zone of genius PLR articles" into Google and see what comes up. If it doesn't show much, play around with other key phrases around your work. You might be surprised with what shows up.

The only industry PLR articles doesn't really work for is... well, writers. This is your area of expertise so go shine with your own prose.

Reaching Your Audience

Creating great content and having a well-oiled, low-priced machine around you to keep that content coming is only valuable when you have an outlet to reach your intended audience.

But before we dive into the three tools that can make a massive difference in your personal brand building endeavors, at a low cost, and within a very quick period of time, we need to address the elephant in the room - and that is all this ridiculous preoccupation with the numbers.

The number of followers you have.
The number of page visits you get to your website.
The number of names on your email list.

These preoccupations can lead you to feel like you've missed the boat, that you aren't relevant enough to gain any traction, that trying to build your audience is going to be impossible, or any number of other potentially limiting thoughts you might think to yourself to justify not spending enough time on building and serving your audience.

However, the number of followers you do or do not have is immaterial to your personal brand building - that's because you are focusing on the wrong metric.

Social media is a relationship management tool, just the same as a telephone or email. All these things can be part of great results - ranging from getting a job offer from a phone interview, to sending an email to a new client. But social media only delivers results that are proportionate to the effort put in. Many, many, people get completely blindsided by vanity metrics that don't make a bit of difference to actually achieving real results.

As an example, I got a call a couple of years ago from a HUGE, I mean massive, global recording artist with well over 60 million fans on Facebook. He said he's leaving Facebook, that it's not worth it. He gets hundreds of thousands of likes but when he gives them a link to something new he is doing or to something that he thinks is important, only 0.002% of his fans click through. I wanted to say 'no s*%t Sherlock, it's because you've conditioned your fans to only want selfies of you. They don't know what you stand for or why you do what you do, so they won't take an action that you recommend.' By contrast, I was working with a celebrity fitness instructor - the fabulous if not a little scary at times - Jillian Michaels, who, at the time, had a million fans. Jillian could post about any number of things and see 80-90,000 people take action. This conversion rate was all because she'd taken the time to form a powerful relationship with her fans where she was less driven by likes, and the number of followers, and more driven by how she could empower each of her followers lives with everything she posts. This mentality was rewarded by heartstring-pulling comments where a follower would pour out their soul telling Jillian how much her work had changed their life. In short, Jillian earned the trust of her followers one person at a time and didn't play the game of grabbing as many fans as she could even if they were the wrong fans.

So, you see, social media is not about the number of fans or followers you have. Here's the big secret that goes against most so-called social media gurus out there, it's not even about the amount of engagement you get, it's about the quality of your followers and your ability to form a connection with them around the unique value proposition of your personal brand (more on how to find your unique value proposition towards the end of this book).

But, let's break this down further. If you're a real estate agent who has a goal of selling 52 homes a year and yet you only had 52 followers, but they all bought a home, would that be a result? Hell yes! If you are an actor who wants your TV show to reach as many people as possible and you only have 50 people following you but they are the top entertainment journalists around the world that, as a result of your tweets, gives your show the attention it deserves and millions of people started to tune in, that would be a result, right? You can make this argument for any industry and any job - even in the extreme, a janitor working at a sports stadium who ends up being followed by a team owner and receiving a promotion as a result of the janitor consistently engaging with the team owner's tweets and posting photos of the stadium.

How many of the 'right' people do you really need to follow you to make a difference in your career? I bet it's a number under 100.

The ROI (return on investment) of a distribution channel is measured by what you get in return for the amount of energy that you put into it. So, my challenge for you today is to actually look at what ROI you want from your content distribution channels and focus on that. I don't want you to focus on the vanity numbers because, as our big fancy recording artist realized all too late, those numbers aren't worth anything.

If you're one of those people that feels a bit uncomfortable with the idea of building a communication strategy to put yourself out there, even though you know there's value in it, this might help. The definition I attribute to a fan or follower (your audience) is someone who sees value in what you have to say because you can provide information and insight that can improve a part of their life. This might include your mom and dad, your friends and yes, those 200 people you've never met but who follow you on

Instagram, but it might not be any of them either. It might be that one person you met at a conference who you spoke to for 5 minutes but left an impression with. By defining fans and followers this way, it frames them as people you can be of service to and not just people that inflate your ego.

Personally, I don't want to grow my fans and followers, I want to grow the number of people I can be of service to. Only by servicing and attracting the 'right' people will I be able to achieve my goals.

With that said, I'm going to dive into the top three tools that I believe will give you the best bang for your buck in building your personal brand. Bare in mind, there are a ton of tools, platforms, and resources that you can use when building your audience - I go into many of these with my online challenges, but for now, let's start with a few of my favorites.

wix.com

Wix is a drag and drop website builder where you can select a template, change out the words and photos, and get your website live all within a few hours - there's no programming or design skills needed.

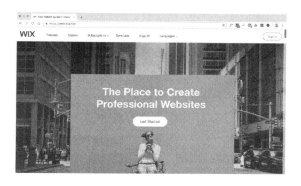

First disclaimer, my website at www.RichardJanes.com is not built on Wix. I designed the website myself, used wordpress with Divi's Visual Drag & Drop Builder, and had assistance from a programmer on Upwork that lives in Serbia. BUT, the first website I built for my personal brand coaching business was on Wix. I built it in 2-3 hours, and within 24 hours it had made me $5,000 from a client who found the site and reached out to me. If you already have a website and you need professional help changing it up or updating basic elements, then the only reason for you to be on that platform is because you are making a good amount of money from it. If you can't go in and update something, you are handicapping how fast you can build your brand and ANYONE has the ability to make basic changes with services like Wix.

Another elephant in the room worthy of addressing - why do you need a website?

One of the first proactive steps you can take in building your brand is to buy your domain name (I use www.godaddy.com for .com and .co.uk domains and then www.marcaria.com for more obscure domains such as www.jan.es which I use as a link shortener to track clicks on my links through https://rebrandly.com/) When my kids were born, I bought their .com domain names, grabbing them before anyone else did. Why? Because we are an internet-driven world.

Just think about how much you use the internet to look up questions, people, and places on any given day. The only place you can have full control over what people see when they look you up is your own website. Perhaps even more importantly, your website is the only place that you can fully capture data around people who look you up. This tracking power can then enable you to build a funnel that potential prospects can go through and where they can dive deeper into your world and the services you have to offer.

Now your website can be as simple or as complex as you like. At its most basic, it's a single page with a photo of you, a short bio, and a link that they can click to contact you. For the purposes of this handbook we are going to presume that is all you need. If you don't have a website under your name already (not your company name, your name!), then don't waste time trying to think about a big fancy website, just get this simple page up today. The great news is that it should only take you a few hours. At some point down the road, you'll be grateful you did.

Now there are many great platforms out there that you can easily build your website on. The two most common are SquareSpace.com and Wix.com. While SquareSpace provides beautiful templates, it doesn't have the same ability to grow as Wix. For this reason, I always point people towards Wix.

Wix has 500+ designer-made website templates that allow you to drag and drop all the elements you need, giving you the power to customize anything you want. However, a quick word of warning, I would advise changing as little as possible. If the sentence structure in the template is four sentences, try and use four sentences. If the photo placeholder they use is a portrait photo, use a portrait photo. The themes have been carefully designed to be balanced, and if you don't take that into consideration as you change up the theme, it will begin to look like a third grader put the website together.

Wix has a very easy blog hosting platform integrated into it which provides access to search engine optimization (SEO) assistive features that optimize your website. This basically means that the search engines can read your content easily which then allows them to send suitable traffic your way.

If you really don't want to get in and play around with building a website, find a template you like, print off the pages, scribble down what you want in each section i.e. write "Change for Text A," and then write the replacement text in a Google doc. Take a photo of all the pages and send those together with the Google doc and a file of your replacement photos to someone on Upwork to make the changes. For approximately $50, you'll have the finished website back to you by morning.

Here's an example of a client who built a simple landing page on Wix:

As you can see, it's nice and simple. The page quickly gets to the point of who he is by telling the website visitor a little story about the value he offers the world. It also includes a couple of links to his representation for additional background. Now, when someone searches for Paul Ruehl, his website is one of the first websites that shows up on Google. He is controlling the initial contact with his brand.

Having a website is one thing, but there's something else that we all have, and very very very (can I say very again), very rarely use, and that's our email list. This rather neatly brings me to the next enormously valuable platform:

Active Campaign.

Active Campaign is my go-to email marketing platform. There are plenty of others out there to explore, with Mailchimp probably being the most well known. Why don't I recommend Mailchimp? Because it's just very basic and won't grow with your business. Whatever platform you use, you'll want it to be able to grow with you as long as possible.

When it comes to building your email list, even if you don't think you do, you already have a ton of contacts. Unless you have just walked out of the jungle, having been lost for the last 25 years, you've been using email for quite some time and have been emailing people in your industry.

Go through ALL your emails, put them ALL into an excel file, save that file as a .csv file, load that file into Active Campaign, and start sending a TON of emails!!!!

NOT SO FAST!

The key is to strategically go through your emails and pull the people who you think will truly value and appreciate your journey, monthly stories, and the information you're going to share with them. Think about it in terms of industry vs. stature, as you'd be surprised by how many high-powered people will actually appreciate you touching base with them every now and again.

Once you have those emails in Active Campaign, the first email should be a short blast letting them know that you are starting a monthly or quarterly newsletter and that you would love to keep them updated on the work you are doing. The initial email should also let them know that if they would like to unsubscribe from the newsletter, they can send a simple reply, leaving no hard feelings. This gives people the opportunity to say they don't want your emails. If this happens, don't take it personally when someone unsubscribes, as people have very full inboxes - it doesn't mean they don't like you anymore!

So why should you be sending emails out and developing a list, especially if you are just building your career vs. actually 'selling' something?

Approximately 99% of us check our email everyday, some as many as 20 times a day. When you compare this to social media where you can completely miss a friend's Facebook update or Instagram pic from their vacation in Italy last month, the chances are that you won't miss an email from them. It's the same with keeping in contact with people who could be instrumental in building your career - from past customers through to vendors, partners, and employers.

Many of my celebrity clients would be all for building an email list consisting of their fans, but they'd never thought about building a separate email list for industry people - journalists, tv execs, agents, managers, etc. - the people who would actually be sending them the work!

A big no-no with your email marketing is to focus on the sales or just the big news. In order for people to keep opening your emails, you need to tell a story with value and unique insight, unique insight that only you can provide.

The underlying goal with a regular email/newsletter is to keep you top of mind. I can't tell you how many times my agency has picked up a $50,000 job from one of our clients because I popped by their office to say hello. Seriously! "Hey, Richard, great to see you. Oh, you know what, you might be able to help with something..." - a regular email (with value) does exactly the same thing.

If you'd like to check out what I consider to be a great example of quality email, check out Kevin Rose's newsletter. He now has over 95,000 subscribers following his journey. You can check it out here: https://www.kevinrose.com/newsletter

Before we move on to the next platform, I want to stress that your newsletter needs to have YOU infused in it's content. It needs to come from you, speak in the first person, and give your insight. Don't go generic on this, as it will fall flat.

With that being said, let's chat about the one social media platform that most people are overlooking, and yet carries value for *everyone* in *every* industry. Are you ready for this...

LinkedIn!

LinkedIn was launched before Facebook, Instagram, Twitter, and Snapchat. In fact, it was launched well before most of the big social media networks that we love to hate today. If there were a living granddaddy of social media, it is them. The reason some might be inclined to dismiss LinkedIn is because originally, it was the place you went when you were looking for a job and... well... that was about it. But, LinkedIn has undergone a massive transformation and now offers a boatload of benefits for you to take advantage of.

Essentially, LinkedIn has evolved to a bonafide content platform. People share status updates, articles, and interact with each other within a business or professional context. The professional context is the key. If you already have a LinkedIn account, even if you haven't used it in years, you will probably have some contacts already waiting to receive great compelling content from you, or at least you'll have a ton of invites that you have largely ignored.

Unlike the other social media platforms, the people you have connections with on LinkedIn tend to be highly targeted connections who are interested in your niche.

Now LinkedIn is still trying to build their name as a "content" platform vs. a "jobs" platform and not enough people have embraced the habit of posting content to their feed. This means that when you post content, there will be a high percentage of your contacts that will see what you have to say.

I have a client who is currently looking for a new job. He works at the top of his industry where most jobs aren't advertised and tend to be filled through people having relationships with board members, etc. The goal was to increase his visibility among the relevant industry stakeholders by regularly sharing his thoughts on his industry and his journey. In doing so, he would be able to remain top of mind among his industry's leaders, which would ideally result in them reaching out with prospective opportunities. It's worth noting that he hadn't really posted to LinkedIn before and had only accepted colleague's invitations as they came up, but nothing more. Over a three week period, he wrote three short articles, posted them on LinkedIn, and had three people reach out to ask if he would be interested in possible job openings, making this initiative a resounding success.

Unlike the other social media platforms, LinkedIn has it's own publishing platform where you can write full blog articles without having a website (which we've established you should at least have a landing page). Even Richard Branson and Bill Gates post long form blogs directly on to LinkedIn.

You may be thinking that LinkedIn still might not be for you, as it's all business. But let me introduce you to Casey Lynn Hancock. Casey is a Los Angeles artist who took to LinkedIn posting photos and videos of herself painting commissions. She was consistent with her posting (one of the biggest factors in success), and her posts began to get crazy engagement with the commissions rolling in.

The only thing I would warn about your LinkedIn content is that you've got to keep it professional. No vacation selfies, no photos of your food, and no nights out with friends.

Of course, there are plenty of other content distribution platforms out there for you to take advantage of, but LinkedIn would be my go-to platform for anyone looking to build their brand and start seeing results in the quickest time possible.

I go into greater detail about how to maximize your results on LinkedIn and build out your presence on other networks in my online "Unlock Your Personal Brand Communication 90-Day Challenge". And this brings me rather neatly to the final set of tools and resources for you to build your influence and dominate your market in rapid time without spending a fortune.

What I am about to introduce you to will save you months of work, help provide you with real clarity on your unique value proposition in the marketplace, and help you can get out of your own way to stand apart from your competition. And you can do this all within just 14-days. 14-days that can change your life...

As an entrepreneur, business owner, or solopreneur trying to build your business, one of the biggest keys to success is being able to speak to what makes you unique over all the other competition out there.

- Why should someone engage you over anyone else?
- Why should someone listen and trust you over anyone else?
- Why should someone give you a career changing opportunity over anyone else?
- Why should you get to charge a premium over anyone else?

Wouldn't it be great to have go-to answers to these questions that you can 100% own, be able to communicate at any moment, and have your answers land whereby the person you are talking to leans forward and wants to know more?

Well the answers to these questions can not be found on a resume.
They can not be found by working years on the job.
They can not be found from recommendations.

The answers to these questions are found in your unique value proposition and how well it connects with your intended audience - that's what truly sets you apart.

I've coached writers of Oscar-winning movies, CEOs of billion-dollar companies, industry thought leaders, college graduates, people from all types of industries going through a period of transition, and everyone in between, on how to speak to *their* unique value proposition and take the next big leap in their career. A leap that many of them thought would be impossible, as they'd been hitting some form of glass ceiling for so long that they'd begun to believe that maybe, just maybe, the dreams they had for themselves where just too big a stretch - that they had been kidding themselves all along.

Their dreams ***were*** within reach.

Your dreams ***are*** within reach.

Now I want to help you break through that ceiling for yourself.

I want to help you get clarity over what makes you unique so that you can start making the type of impact you know, deep down, you are capable of.

I want to help you get closer to realizing your dreams than ever before.

With this 14-day online challenge, you are just a few short steps away from opening a box that can never be closed again. A box that will fill you with confidence and give you the clarity of mind to take the next big step in your journey and fully utilize all the tools we've been talking about in this book.

I know how busy you are. The fact that you've sat down to read this book is fantastic and goes to show how committed you are to upping your game. Because I understand how busy you are, I've built this 14-day challenge specifically for you.

On the first Monday of each month I open the doors for a new group to take the challenge. If you're finally at the point where you're ready to take the next big step in your career (and by extension your life), and you sign up to the challenge, I'll send you a short 5-15 minute video to watch each day with your morning coffee. Each video is accompanied by a short worksheet that you can either complete there and then or work on throughout the day when time allows.

Through these videos, I'll take you on a guided journey to identify the three words of your Unique Value Proposition (UVP) and show you how your new found UVP can be applied throughout your life to open up more opportunities to achieve those big audacious hairy dreams that keep you up at night.

Everyone can find just 20 minutes in the morning, or perhaps it's 20 minutes before you go to bed, to watch a video and complete a brief worksheet - that's seriously all it takes! If you have a partner or kids, involve them too, they will thank you for it, just as mine have done.

Bottom line, for the rest of your life you'll be able to call upon the three words of your UVP to give you resolve and confidence as you face the world.

I'll then show you how you can communicate your UVP in a carefully chosen response so that next time someone asks, 'What do you do?,' you'll have an answer that will open up the sort of opportunities that you have been looking for.

You'll bring a new found focus to how you're showing up throughout your life, understanding precisely where you're able to have the most impact on those around you. This will de-escalate any anxiety and agitation you are feeling about personal and professional value.

That said, I'm asking you something right now that I really want you to consider very, very seriously.

What would happen to you if you made the same strategic and tactical shifts in both your business and personal life that I have?

What would it be like to confidently be putting yourself out there more?

Think about that for a minute.

What if you no longer had to second guess what to do and you just did it?

Well I've got the roadmap and blueprints ready for you to feel this and it all starts with the Unlock Your Personal Brand Power 14-Day Challenge.

Now the ball's in your court. You could be in a very different position in just 14-days, how about that?

Head on over to:

www.UnlockYourPersonalBrandPower.com

And take the next big step in your career.

I'm so excited for you,

Richard James

Made in the USA
Lexington, KY
07 November 2019